SOUTH RIVER MEDIA

JAMES MONROE

The Presidents of the United States

George Washington
1789–1797

John Adams
1797–1801

Thomas Jefferson
1801–1809

James Madison
1809–1817

James Monroe
1817–1825

John Quincy Adams
1825–1829

Andrew Jackson
1829–1837

Martin Van Buren
1837–1841

William Henry Harrison
1841

John Tyler
1841–1845

James Polk
1845–1849

Zachary Taylor
1849–1850

Millard Fillmore
1850–1853

Franklin Pierce
1853–1857

James Buchanan
1857–1861

Abraham Lincoln
1861–1865

Andrew Johnson
1865–1869

Ulysses S. Grant
1869–1877

Rutherford B. Hayes
1877–1881

James Garfield
1881

Chester Arthur
1881–1885

Grover Cleveland
1885–1889

Benjamin Harrison
1889–1893

Grover Cleveland
1893–1897

William McKinley
1897–1901

Theodore Roosevelt
1901–1909

William H. Taft
1909–1913

Woodrow Wilson
1913–1921

Warren Harding
1921–1923

Calvin Coolidge
1923–1929

Herbert Hoover
1929–1933

Franklin D. Roosevelt
1933–1945

Harry Truman
1945–1953

Dwight Eisenhower
1953–1961

John F. Kennedy
1961–1963

Lyndon Johnson
1963–1969

Richard Nixon
1969–1974

Gerald Ford
1974–1977

Jimmy Carter
1977–1981

Ronald Reagan
1981–1989

George H. W. Bush
1989–1993

William J. Clinton
1993–2001

George W. Bush
2001–2009

Presidents and Their Times

JAMES MONROE

CORINNE J. NADEN AND ROSE BLUE

Marshall Cavendish
Benchmark
New York

Marshall Cavendish Benchmark
99 White Plains Road
Tarrytown, New York 10591-5502
www.marshallcavendish.us

All Internet sites were correct at the time of printing.

Library of Congress Cataloging-in-Publication Data

Naden, Corinne J.
James Monroe / by Corinne J. Naden and Rose Blue.
p. cm. — (Presidents and their times)
Summary: "Provides comprehensive information on President James Monroe and places him
within his historical and cultural context. Also explored are the formative events of his times
and how he responded"—Provided by publisher.
Includes bibliographical references and index.
ISBN 978-0-7614-2838-1
1. Monroe, James, 1758–1831—Juvenile literature. 2. Presidents—United States—Biography—Juvenile
literature. 3. United States—Politics and government—1817–1825—Juvenile literature. I. Blue, Rose. II.
Title.
E372.N33 2008
973.5'4092—dc22
[B]
2007029480

Editor: Christine Florie
Publisher: Michelle Bisson
Art Director: Anahid Hamparian
Series Designer: Alex Ferrari

Photo research by Connie Gardner

Cover photo by James Monroe(1758–1831)(colour litho), Morse, Samuel, F. B. (1791–1872)/Private
Collection, Peter Newark American Pictures/The Bridgeman Art Library.

The photographs in this book are used by permission and through the courtesy of: *The Granger Collection:*
3, 8, 24, 27, 29, 33, 40, 53, 56, 63, 65, 67, 69, 74, 76, 80, 85, 86(L), 86(R), 87(R); *The Bridgeman Art
Library:* Voting in Philadelphia, 1816 (w/c on paper), American School (19th century)/Private Collection,
Peter Newark American Pictures, 6; The Fight on Lexington Common, April 19, 1775, from The Story
of the Revolution by Woodrow Wilson (1856–1924); published in Scribner's Magazine, January 3, 1898
(oil on canvas) by Howard Pyle (1853–1911) c Delaware Art Museum, Wilmington, USA/Howard Pyle
Collection, 15; *Getty Images:* Hulton Archive, 9, 78; *The Image Works:* Topham, 20; *North Wind Picture
Archive:* 11, 13, 26, 42, 43, 49, 72; *Corbis:* Bettmann, 17, 46, 48, 51, 55; CORBIS: 31, 60, 82;
Art Archive: Culver Pictures, 28, 37, 54, 87 (L).

Printed in Malaysia
1 3 5 6 4 2

CONTENTS

Residents of Philadelphia take to the streets to vote during the presidential election of 1816.

THE LAD FROM VIRGINIA

One

*J*ames Monroe became president of the United States when the national mood was good. The year was 1816 and the Era of Good Feelings was just beginning. Two years earlier, in 1814, the War of 1812 with Great Britain ended with a peace treaty. The United States did not win the war, but it did win some important battles. Americans were feeling good because they had stood up to the mighty British forces. Now the country was at peace. There were no serious problems with other nations. There were no large fights among political leaders at home. All these good feelings came upon James Monroe as he entered the presidency.

Early in Monroe's presidency, he and his wife, Elizabeth, toured the New England states of Connecticut and Massachusetts. People waved and cheered wherever they went. Boston's July 12, 1817 *Columbian Centinel* called the trip "an era of good feelings." That phrase stuck throughout most of Monroe's years in office. He was so popular that he would run unopposed for a second term in 1820.

James Monroe was the country's last great leader of the eighteenth century. His energy, enthusiasm, and passion made him the Republican Party's choice for president. While president, his introduction of the Monroe Doctrine established the United States as independent to European nations. His national policies, together with his foreign policies, offered him much success as president.

CHILDHOOD

James Monroe was born April 28, 1758, on a plantation in Westmoreland County, Virginia, in an area called the Northern Neck. His father and mother, Spence and Elizabeth Jones Monroe, were neither rich nor poor. They farmed about 500 acres and were known as **landed gentry**. Cattle were raised on the Monroe plantation, and corn, barley, and tobacco were grown.

The Monroe family came to America from Scotland in the mid-seventeenth century. Monroe's mother's ancestors were from Wales. Monroe had three younger brothers, Andrew, Spence, and Joseph Jones, and an older sister, Elizabeth. Very little else is known about his family. Monroe grew up like other young men on southern plantations at the time. He liked hunting and fishing and the outdoors. Even though he became president, Monroe always thought of himself as a farmer.

James Monroe was born in this farmhouse in Westmoreland County, Virginia in 1758.

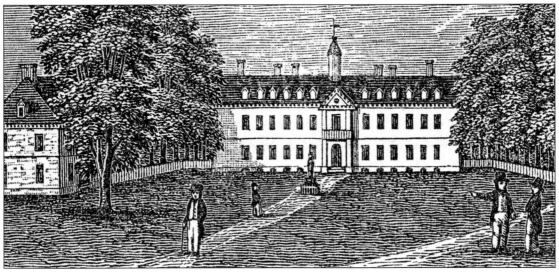

James Monroe studied at the College of William and Mary as the colonies prepared to battle with Great Britain.

EDUCATION

When Monroe was eleven years old, he began to study at Campbelltown Academy, several miles from his home. He walked a long way to school each day. Campbelltown was a highly regarded school run by Parson Archibald Campbell, a strict Scotsman. Monroe learned Latin, literature, math, and science from Campbell. In 1774, at age sixteen, Monroe entered the College of William and Mary in Williamsburg, Virginia. As the colonies were gaining ground to enter war with Great Britain, the young James Monroe found it difficult to focus on his education. However, he stayed at William and Mary for more than a year. During that time, his father died. His uncle, Judge Joseph Jones, oversaw Monroe's education and became his guardian and top adviser. The judge wanted his young nephew to prepare for a career in politics.

School Days

James Monroe attended the second-oldest school of higher education in the United States. Only Harvard University in Cambridge, Massachusetts, is older than the College of William and Mary, which was chartered in 1693. (Harvard was chartered in 1636.) King William III and Queen Mary II of England granted the charter to train clergymen in the British colonies, which later became the United States of America. The Sir Christopher Wren Building on the college campus—built in 1695—is the nation's oldest school building in continuous use. Besides Monroe, two other presidents attended William and Mary: Thomas Jefferson and John Tyler.

Talk of War

Between 1607 and 1732 Great Britain founded thirteen colonies in North America. Through the years, there was more and more trouble between the colonists—including Monroe's own family—and the royal government. A major quarrel was over taxes. More and more, the quarrels turned to violence.

In 1765 Great Britain issued the Stamp Act. The act ensured that money was collected from the colonies by taxing such things as newspapers and pamphlets. Monroe's father and grandfather were among those who protested. The colonists were so angry over the new tax that they started riots and burned stamps.

Angry colonists protest the taxing of paper goods enforced by Great Britain's Stamp Act.

British merchants began to complain that the rioting was hurting their business, so the Stamp Act was **repealed** in 1766. The colonists began to talk of freedom, even if it would lead to war with Great Britain. It was still just talk at this stage, but young Monroe easily became caught up in the excitement.

In 1770 British troops fired on a crowd of local workers in Boston, Massachusetts, who were taunting them. Five colonists died in what is known as the Boston Massacre. In 1773 American patriots dressed themselves as Native Americans, boarded British ships in Boston Harbor, and dumped the cargo of tea overboard to protest the tax on tea. Their cry was "no taxation without representation." The colonists protested because although they had to pay taxes, they had no say in passing the tax laws that governed them.

The relationship between England and the colonies became even more strained after the Boston Tea Party. King George III had Parliament pass the Coercive Acts in 1774, which among other things closed the port of Boston, threatening the very life of the port city.

Frustrated and ever more defiant, colonists set up the First **Continental Congress** in September 1774. **Delegates** from each of the colonies met in Philadelphia to discuss the growing problems. They petitioned King George with a letter signed by the delegates that listed their grievances. King George's response was to ignore their plea.

Soon, talk of war became a fight for freedom. In March 1775 Virginia's Patrick Henry spoke to the Second Virginia Convention in Richmond. Henry was a fiery and brilliant speaker. By now he was certain that there would be war between Great Britain and

One of the Coercive Acts passed in 1774 allowed British soldiers to quarter in American colonist's homes.

the colonies. He wanted to arm the Virginia militia for the coming fight. Henry said, "I know not what course others may take, but as for me, give me liberty or give me death!"

THE SHOT HEARD 'ROUND THE WORLD

Less than a month after Henry's liberty-or-death speech, the war for American independence began. It started with skirmishes

COERCIVE ACTS OF 1774

Also known as the Intolerable Acts, the Coercive Acts were passed to punish the colonists for protests such as the Boston Tea Party. Five punishments were introduced, but only four were directed at the colonies. The first act closed the port of Boston until the colonists paid for the tea they destroyed. The second act reduced Massachusetts to a crown colony, which meant it would be ruled by a military governor. There was still a legislative assembly, but the colonists could not hold town meetings without British approval. The third act forced British officials charged with crimes to return to England for trial. The fourth act allowed British troops to be housed in occupied American homes.

The fifth act, the Quebec Act, removed all territory between the Ohio and Mississippi rivers from colonial rule. The region was given to the Province of Quebec. These measures were Great Britain's attempt to appease the new British citizens of Quebec, formerly Frenchmen.

between British soldiers and colonists at the Battles of Lexington and Concord in Massachusetts.

General Thomas Gage, a British commander, had recently been appointed royal governor of Massachusetts. It was his job to enforce the Coercive Acts. Gage received information that the colonists were storing gunpowder and military supplies at Concord. On the night of April 18, 1775, he sent some seven hundred men to seize it. But patriot Paul Revere and two other messengers had already ridden through the night warning the colonists that "the British are coming."

In the early morning mist of April 19, British troops marched into the village of Lexington. There they were met by about seventy armed colonists known as minutemen. No one knows who fired the first shot, but in a few moments eight colonists were dead. The British troops moved on to Concord. It was there that the colonist farmers "fired the shot heard 'round the world," immortalized in "Concord Hymn," a poem by Ralph Waldo Emerson.

Howard Pyle recreated the infamous battle scene that took place between British troops and American colonists at Lexington, Massachusetts.

Feeling victorious, the British began the march back to Boston. All along the road, their bright red coats became the target of the colonists. By the time the British returned they had suffered almost three times more casualties than the colonists. The American Revolution had begun.

GOING TO WAR

The words of Patrick Henry and news of the battles spread throughout the colonies. Early in 1776 the Continental Congress called for "expert riflemen" companies to be formed in Pennsylvania, Maryland, and Virginia.

The call from the Continental Congress was enough for Monroe. He left college with a few of his friends to join the Third Virginia Regiment of Foot. He was now seventeen years old. Monroe was large-framed, about 6-feet tall, and a rather homely lad, except for his striking eyes. He was also an expert rifleman. He was assigned to a company and given the standard uniform of a fringed hunting shirt, a three-cornered cocked hat, and a rifle. As an adult, Monroe was thoughtful, modest, serious, and somewhat shy. But at this age he was bubbling over with excitement for the cause of revolution.

His excitement reached a new pitch when the big news reached Williamsburg that the Declaration of Independence was adopted by the Continental Congress on July 4, 1776. It was largely the work of Thomas Jefferson. The Declaration formally announced the separation of the thirteen American colonies from Great Britain.

Monroe, who quickly became a lieutenant, spent time practicing rifle drills on the lawns of Williamsburg. Then in August came the call to battle. The seven hundred-man Third Regiment marched north from Virginia to New York. By the time the regiment arrived in Manhattan, General George Washington was about to lose New York City to the British. Monroe's first battle was in Harlem Heights in the northern part of the city in mid-September. The smaller Virginia force suffered heavy losses but held its ground against the British until reinforcements arrived.

In December Washington decided to take his battered army across the Delaware River into Pennsylvania from New Jersey. They crossed the Delaware to look for British troops in Trenton, New Jersey. Before the crossing, on Christmas Eve, Monroe and a captain scouted the enemy camp, which was manned by Hessian troops—German soldiers who fought with the British for a

In a much needed defeat, George Washington's troops surprised Hessian soldiers at Trenton, New Jersey, in December 1776.

fee. On the night of December 25, Washington and his men crossed the ice-clogged Delaware and met with Monroe, who reported a drunken party in the British camp. With that news, Washington decided to attack at dawn. The raid was successful and a much-needed morale booster for the Americans.

Lieutenant Monroe was severely wounded in the battle for Trenton. A musket ball landed near the base of his neck. Without the swift action of a surgeon in the field, he probably would have bled to death. As it was, it took him about three months to recover. The musket ball remained in his shoulder for the rest of his life. For that bravery he was promoted to captain. Monroe was not quite nineteen years old.

MISERY AND DEFEAT

When Monroe recovered he was assigned as an aide to William Alexander, Lord Stirling. One of Washington's commanders, Stirling was American-born but claimed a Scottish earldom. Being an aide largely meant carrying messages and keeping records. However, Monroe did take part in the battles of Brandywine and Germantown while serving with Stirling.

On September 11, 1777, Stirling's brigade was pinned down at Brandywine Creek in southeastern Pennsylvania. Although the British won the battle, they did not destroy Washington's army or cut it off from the revolutionary capital at Philadelphia. That allowed the Americans to fight on.

During the battle Monroe stopped to help Marquis de Lafayette, a French nobleman who was wounded. Lafayette had left a life of ease and privilege in France to join the fight for freedom in America. At the age of nineteen, Lafayette was given the rank of major general. His wounds at Brandywine were not

Army Life As an Aide

Most of Monroe's duties as Lord Stirling's aide were tedious. When not carrying messages or keeping records, he accompanied the commander on his rounds. This may have been boring at times, but it was by no means a safe job. Stirling was a soldier who liked to stay close to his men. That usually meant being in the field with them. And that meant that he, as well as Monroe, was almost constantly exposed to enemy fire.

serious and he soon recovered. After that battle, Monroe and Lafayette became lifelong friends.

The following month, on October 4, Monroe was part of another defeat for the Continental troops. It took place in Germantown, north of Philadelphia. Washington drew up a complicated battle plan, but it failed partly because of dense fog that morning. After that, Washington led about ten thousand regulars to spend a terrible winter at Valley Forge, Pennsylvania. Beginning about December 19, 1777, the weather became a test of discipline and morale over severe hardship. The weather that winter was extremely harsh. Because of the awful conditions and lack of food, disease swept the camp. Perhaps as many as three thousand died, and many were ill.

Despite the dreadful winter, the Americans marched out of Valley Forge in June 1778 as a well-disciplined fighting force. This was due to Washington's leadership and the drilling methods

After fighting several difficult battles, Washington wintered his ragged army at Valley Forge, Pennsylvania.

introduced by Baron Friedrich von Steuben, former captain in the Prussian army. Congress assigned him to train the troops at Valley Forge. The drill company that he formed became a model for the entire Continental army. Von Steuben himself earned the title of major general.

On June 19 Monroe, now a captain, and the others left Valley Forge on a slow march north to Monmouth, New Jersey. Both sides claimed victory at Monmouth on June 28, 1778. It was Monroe's last battle.

BACK TO VIRGINIA

For some time Monroe had wanted to form his own command, but after Monmouth, he was one of many Continental officers who were retired. Monroe left the army as a lieutenant colonel at the age of twenty. However, the war was not yet over. Monroe decided to return home to join the Virginia militia and recruit his own volunteers. Washington even wrote a rare letter of praise for him:

> *I very sincerely lament that the situation of our service will not permit us to do justice to the merits of Major Monroe. . . . It is with pleasure I take occasion to express to you the high opinion I have of his worth. . . . He has, in every instance, maintained the reputation of a brave, active, and sensible officer.*

Monroe did get his **commission** for a command in the militia, but there were just too few volunteers left in the colony to fill it. Washington later praised Monroe for his bravery during the war.

When Monroe was in Williamsburg still waiting for a command, he met Virginia's governor, Thomas Jefferson. The two became lifelong friends. Jefferson appointed Monroe as a military commissioner. It was his job to develop a communication system that could warn of the advancement of British troops north from the Carolinas. Monroe spent several months traveling through the southern colonies to gather news about the movements of the British forces. Jefferson also encouraged the young Monroe to think about his future career. He suggested the study of law.

LAWYER AND LEGISLATOR

$\mathcal{F}$resh from military service, young James Monroe was undecided about his future. But both his uncle Judge Joseph Jones and his friend Thomas Jefferson had encouraged him to study law. One possibility was for him to return to the College of William and Mary, where he had the chance to study under George Wythe, called the nation's finest legal mind. But Monroe chose another fine mind to shape his future. He would study law with Jefferson. At that time many students would "read the law" with an established attorney rather than attend college. Even though Jefferson was Virginia's governor, he did accept a few law students.

LEARNING THE LAW

At Jefferson's suggestion, Monroe followed him to Richmond when the new Virginia capital was moved there in 1780. Monroe sold his property in Westmoreland County. He moved to a small estate in King George County to complete his studies. Jefferson's method of teaching was to have his students study reports of cases that had already been decided. Then the students were required to write their own report on each case.

Thomas Jefferson had a great influence on James Monroe, both as a man and as a politician. It was not unusual for Jefferson to encourage younger men when he discovered outstanding

Thomas Jefferson (right) was a great inspiration to Monroe and guided him toward the study of law.

qualities in them. Monroe needed that encouragement, for when he left the army, he had no idea what to do with his future. Monroe could not equal Jefferson in intellectual brilliance, as few could, but Jefferson applauded the warmth and goodness and the sound thinking of the younger man. As for Monroe, he had the rare opportunity to learn from one of the liveliest and most informed minds of the period.

After British General Charles Cornwallis surrendered his troops at Yorktown, Virginia, in October 1781, the war was all but over. (It ended formally with the Treaty of Paris, signed on September 3, 1783. Great Britain recognized the independence of the United States with western boundaries that extended to the Mississippi River.) Monroe now thought he might act on a plan that he had been thinking of for some time. He would complete his education abroad. Jefferson agreed, even though he did not generally recommend foreign study for Americans. Jefferson even wrote Monroe a letter of recommendation to the American Peace Commissioners in Paris. But all the planning proved fruitless because Monroe was unable to obtain ship passage. He would have to find something to do at home.

ENTERING POLITICS

Deciding against more education, Monroe did find something to do at home. In 1782 he began a political career in Virginia. At the age of twenty-four, he was elected to the Virginia Assembly. He took the seat of his uncle, who had recently been named as a delegate to the Continental Congress. Membership in the assembly was important because it gave Monroe a chance to be recognized by the most powerful and established men in the state.

Monroe's political career began in the Virginia Assembly among some of the most influential men in the state.

During his year in the assembly, Monroe allied himself with the strong conservative faction, men such as George Mason, James Madison, and his uncle Judge Joseph Jones. These were the people mainly concerned with strengthening the Union. In 1783 he was elected to Congress under the Articles of Confederation. Over the next three years he pressed for free navigation on the Mississippi River and fought for granting western lands to veterans of the Revolution. His proposal that the Congress should have the authority to regulate foreign and interstate commerce later became part of the U.S. Constitution. Monroe also suggested that perhaps Great Britain might be persuaded to sell Canada to the United States.

In 1786 Monroe was admitted to the Virginia bar and practiced law in Fredericksburg while still in politics. He married Elizabeth Kortright that year. He was a member of the Virginia Ratifiying Convention in 1788, which was convened to accept or reject the new country's constitution. Monroe voted against **ratification**. He felt, as did others such as Jefferson and Madison, that the Constitution gave the federal government too much power over the states. Monroe feared the power of direct taxation that the Constitu-

Monroe's early years in politics proved his ability and strength in moving America toward independence.

tion gave to Congress. This fear was somewhat modified by the figure of George Washington, whom all of the leaders felt would never abuse such power. The Bill of Rights, the first ten amendments to the Constitution, was later added to ensure that powers of the people would be protected.

When the Constitution was ratified, Monroe, despite his reservations, supported it. When slavery was brought up at the convention, he had nothing to say. Like many Virginians of his time, he was torn by the slavery issue. All his life, Monroe owned slaves, and yet he believed that the institution of slavery was wrong.

MARRIAGE

The same year he was admitted to the bar, 1786, Monroe married seventeen-year-old Elizabeth Kortright of New York City. He had met her a year earlier in New York when he was attending the Continental Congress. The daughter of a merchant who had lost his fortune, she was a young lady of much grace and beauty. Chronically ill for most of her adult life, Elizabeth showed such formal manners in public that some thought her cold and reserved. She preferred to stay away from social functions. A somewhat shy man himself, Monroe often demonstrated great pride in his lovely wife. The couple would have two daughters, Eliza, born in 1786, and Maria Hester, born in 1803. A son, James Spence, was born in 1799, but died in 1800.

POLITICAL PARTIES

Turning his full attention to politics again, Monroe ran for a seat in the House of Representatives in 1788. James Madison, who would become the nation's fourth president, beat him by a substantial margin. Jefferson had earlier introduced the two men and now they became friends. Two years later, at the age of thirty-two, Monroe won a seat in the Senate. He joined the Senate in Philadelphia, which was the seat of government at the time.

There, he was reunited with his friends Jefferson and Madison. Jefferson was now the nation's first secretary of state in the administration of George Washington.

During the very early years of the young nation, there were no political parties as we know them today. Many of the nation's leaders were opposed to them. Washington thought that political parties, such as in Great Britain, were a corrupting influence. He felt that people should forget their differences and enact laws strictly for the good of the country, not for personal gain.

Despite such feelings, by the end of Washington's first term, political parties began to emerge when groups began to disagree,

THE

FEDERALIST:

ADDRESSED TO THE

PEOPLE OF THE STATE OF
NEW-YORK.

NUMBER I.

Introduction.

AFTER an unequivocal experience of the inefficacy of the subsisting federal government, you are called upon to deliberate on a new constitution for the United States of America. The subject speaks its own importance ; comprehending in its consequences, nothing less than the existence of the UNION, the safety and welfare of the parts of which it is composed, the fate of an empire, in many respects, the most interesting in the world. It has been frequently remarked, that it seems to have been reserved to the people of this country, by their conduct and example, to decide the important question, whether societies of men are really capable or not, of establishing good government from reflection and choice, or whether they are forever destined to depend, for their political constitutions, on accident and force. If there be any truth in the remark, the crisis, at which we are arrived, may with propriety be regarded as the æra in which

A   that

Written by Alexander Hamilton in 1788, The Federalist *addressed the belief in a federal constitution.*

despite Washington's hopes. Names were given to the opposing sides. Monroe, Jefferson, Madison, and others began to unite against the policies of the so-called **Federalists**. The Federalists were led by Alexander Hamilton, secretary of the treasury. Like Washington and John Adams, Hamilton believed in a strong, centralized federal government. The **Anti-Federalists** were afraid that such a government would control too much power, which could eventually lead to abuse. These Anti-Federalists came to be called Democratic-Republicans.

Trouble in Paris

In 1789 the people of France overthrew Louis XVI during the French Revolution. Washington knew that Monroe admired the leaders of the French Revolution. Monroe knew the president did not share his feelings. Even so, Monroe was not the president's first choice as minister to France. Robert R. Livingston, first secretary of the Department of Foreign Affairs, and James Madison were offered the position but both refused. Washington then turned to Monroe. That put the senator in a somewhat uncomfortable spot. Monroe knew that he might find himself disagreeing with his own administration. But he felt it was his duty to accept the post.

The Voyage to Paris

Sailing to Paris with Monroe were his wife, eight-year-old daughter Eliza, and two servants, Michael and Polly. Monroe's fifteen-year-old cousin, Joseph Jones Jr., accompanied them to complete his education abroad. The voyage took about one month over calm seas. The cost was $700, $400 for the cabins and $300 for supplies. Monroe had also purchased sugar and hams before boarding, as they were said to be scarce in Paris.

Monroe was probably not pleased about having to pay the added cost of the sugar and hams. In those early years, American leaders paid most of their expenses out of their own pockets.

Washington wanted Monroe to leave at once. Not even returning to Virginia, Monroe quickly arranged for his two brothers to take care of the plantation at home. In mid-June of 1794, about three weeks after his appointment, Monroe, his wife, and daughter Eliza set sail for France out of Baltimore.

Before Monroe reached Paris, another U.S. diplomat, John Jay, was already at work in London, the start of Monroe's trouble.

In 1794 Monroe and his family set sail from Baltimore Harbor (above) to France to fulfill his appointment as minister to that country.

Diplomat Jay was also the first chief justice of the U.S. Supreme Court. Washington sent him to England to negotiate a new treaty that would be a giant step for the United States in building a sound national economy. Jay's treaty, formally known as the Treaty of Amity, Commerce, and Navigation, was signed on November 19, 1794. It set up better trade relations between the two countries. Great Britain would pay **damages** for its attacks on U.S. shipping. It agreed to leave the Northwest Territory by June 1, 1796. The British had occupied much of this land before the revolution. The Northwest Territory eventually became the states of Illinois, Indiana, Michigan, Ohio, Wisconsin, and a small part of Minnesota. The treaty also said that the Mississippi River was open to both countries, an important factor for U.S. growth. At the time, the young United States did not extend beyond the Mississippi.

However, Secretary of State Edmund Randolph did not tell Monroe about the new treaty with Great Britain. The new French minister was not warmly received in Paris. In fact, it took a few days before anyone would even see him. Maximilien Robespierre, one of the radical leaders of the French Revolution, had just been executed. The Jacobin government was still annoyed at having to dismiss the previous U.S. minister. And it was not at all sure that it could trust the United States.

THE PRO-FRENCH SPEECH

Finally, Monroe was called in to see the French leaders. He tried to convince them that Jay's talks in London were no threat to France. Monroe believed what he said because he did not know about the new treaty. However, he did know that the U.S. government did

As minister to France, Monroe met with French leaders to assure them that Washington's administration was of no threat to them.

not feel all that kindly toward the French Revolution. He knew that Washington was adamant about U.S. neutrality, but Monroe could not resist letting his own feelings take over. He delivered a very pro-French speech. He spoke of how much the two countries were alike. He spoke of the noble French Revolution. He spoke of the bravery of the French troops. Said Monroe:

> *America had her day of oppression, difficulty and war, but her reasons were virtuous and brave and the storm, which long clouded her political horizon has passed and left them in the enjoyment of peace, liberty and independence. France . . . has now embarked in the same noble career; and I am happy to add that whilst the fortitude, magnanimity and heroic valor her troops command the admiration and applause of the astonished world, the wisdom and firmness of her councils unite equally in securing the happiest result.*

All this showed far more warmth from the American government than Monroe knew to be true. When news of the speech traveled across the ocean to America, Secretary of State Edmund Randolph was displeased.

But that was nothing compared to the French reaction when they finally heard that Jay had signed the new treaty with England. They were outraged. The treaty said to France that the United States had no intention of remaining neutral.

Monroe's government was unhappy with him because of his speech. Monroe was unhappy with his government because he had not been told of Jay's treaty. At first he had hopes that the Senate would reject it. However, it was passed by both houses of Congress. After the treaty was ratified in June 1795, the French said it ruined their commercial pact with the United States, signed in 1778. So, French ships began to attack American ships, which would later lead to an undeclared naval war.

By 1796 Timothy Pickering, a staunch Federalist, had replaced Randolph as secretary of state. Pickering was not at all happy with Monroe's performance in France and wanted him removed. After two years as a diplomat, Monroe came home.

Regardless of the Jay treaty, Monroe had to share some of the blame for his recall. Instead of representing the views of his government, he let his own beliefs take control.

While in France Monroe began to look at the future of the United States. He saw the young country growing into a world power that must live in peace and harmony with other world powers. This vision inspired him to encourage the growth of the United States during his future years in government.

FROM GOVERNOR TO THE CABINET

Three

Monroe was now without a job and unhappy with his recall from France. He was, however, pleased to continue his friendship with Thomas Jefferson, who was now the vice president in the administration of John Adams (1797–1801). Adams and Jefferson were on different sides of the political fence. At that time the idea of political parties was still very new. The positions of president and vice president went to the two people who received the highest votes, regardless of party. That is how Adams, a Federalist, and Jefferson, a Republican, ended up heading the government.

As a sign of Jefferson's continuing trust and friendship, the vice president met Monroe's ship when he returned from France. Even though Monroe was pleased at the sign of trust, he felt he had done no wrong in his diplomatic service. In fact, Pickering had never pointed out in detail the reasons for his recall. So, Monroe went back to Virginia and wrote his own defense. He gave it a rather long title: *A View of the Conduct of the Executive, in the Foreign Affairs of the United States Connected with the Mission to the French Republic During the Years 1794, 5 & 6.*

Monroe did not criticize Washington personally, but he did criticize the foreign policy of the president's administration. In his own defense, he said that the United States was going against its own best interests with an anti-French policy, "the friendship of a nation lost, the most powerful on earth, who had deserved better things from us. . . . Long will it be before we shall be able to forget what we are, nor will centuries suffice to raise us to the high ground from which we have fallen."

As expected, Federalists condemned the work and Republicans praised it. After that experience, Monroe thought about seeking reelection to Congress. Then he heard that his name was suggested as the Republican candidate for governor of Virginia. Since Republicans controlled the state legislature, his election seemed a sure thing.

GOVERNOR

Monroe ran for governor of Virginia and was elected over Federalist James Breckenridge in December 1799. During the campaign, Madison defended Monroe when criticisms arose over his diplomatic career. Monroe served three one-year terms, the maximum allowed.

By design, the governor's position in Virginia was weak. Monroe tried unsuccessfully to bring reforms to state laws. He appealed to the legislature to increase money for public education. He was successful, however, in putting down a slave revolt to take place in Richmond. This was a complex situation for him, a slaveowner who recognized the injustices of the institution.

James Monroe served as governor to the state of Virginia from 1799 to 1802.

SLAVE REVOLT

The first major slave revolt in U.S. history was planned by Gabriel, a deeply religious, Virginia-born slave. He recruited about one thousand slaves, although some experts say the figure was much higher. Gabriel planned a march on Richmond in August 1800. Monroe sent out the state militia and captured Gabriel and the others. They were hanged. The attempted revolt was over, but it greatly increased southerners' fear of the slaves they owned.

THE LOUISIANA PURCHASE

When Monroe retired as governor in 1802, he set up a law practice in Richmond. As usual, he was short of money, and private practice paid more than public office. But after a short time as a private lawyer, Monroe was back in the diplomatic business. This time, he was called to duty by President Thomas Jefferson.

Jefferson asked Monroe to join Robert R. Livingston, minister to France, in Paris as a special **envoy**. Understanding that Monroe might not want to leave his private practice, Jefferson called on him to make a temporary sacrifice. Monroe still knew some of the French leaders and had worked with them. Monroe accepted the post and became involved in the greatest land bargain in U.S. history.

In March 1803 the young nation consisted of seventeen states. Settlers were streaming westward into the valleys of the Tennessee and Ohio rivers. If the United States were to grow, settlers had to be given the right to use the Mississippi River for transportation. They also had to ship goods through the port of New Orleans in the Louisiana Territory. Back in 1795 Spain owned the territory of Louisiana and its port. The Spanish had granted shipping rights through the mouth of the Mississippi. But in 1800 Napoleon had the Spanish king give the territory back to France, which had previously owned it.

Jefferson was afraid that France might now take over absolute control of the mouth of the Mississippi. France was a much stronger possible enemy than Spain.

When Monroe arrived in Paris, Livingston was already deep in talks with the French leaders about Louisiana and the Mississippi River. Monroe carried a message from Jefferson. It warned that the talks might fail if the United States did not secure at least some part of New Orleans to ensure shipping through the Gulf of Mexico.

To the surprise of Livingston and Monroe, French government leaders said that Napoleon was thinking about selling the *entire* Louisiana Territory to the United States. Napoleon apparently made the offer for three reasons. The first was that the French had suffered a slave revolt on the island of Haiti in the West Indies. They no longer felt secure about holding territory in the Americas. Second, Napoleon feared that France and England were nearing war again, and he needed money to rebuild his army. And third, Napoleon was not certain how large the Louisiana Territory was.

The price for the sale was $15,000,000 for what turned out to be about 828,000 square miles. That came to about three cents

In April 1803
Monroe traveled to
France to negotiate,
with French leaders,
the purchase of the
Louisiana Territory.

an acre. Neither Livingston nor Monroe had authority to make the purchase, nor were they authorized to pay that much. However, they realized the importance of the opportunity. They also knew that to inform the United States of the sale and to have Congress vote on it would take too much time. Another country might acquire the land. So, they bought the Louisiana Territory and returned home.

President Jefferson was somewhat alarmed when he received the news. He believed in a strict interpretation of the Constitution, which did not give the country the power to acquire new land. But after careful thought and debate with others, the president approved the sale.

The purchase of the Louisiana Territory is sometimes considered the biggest accomplishment of Jefferson's administration. It was unclear, however, just what had been bought. The wording of the treaty was vague and no boundaries were fixed.

MONROE IN FRANCE

Monroe spent four months in France on the matter of the Louisiana Purchase. During that time, he renewed some old friendships. He visited Lafayette, whom he had not seen in twenty years, now confined at home with a broken hip. Monroe was particularly pleased to deliver to Lafayette an act of Congress that gave the Revolutionary hero some western lands for his services.

This map illustrates the United States after the purchase of the Louisiana Territory in 1803.

Actually, the United States had nearly doubled in size. Livingston was the diplomat who did most of the negotiating with France for the treaty, but it helped Monroe's career at home because his signature was also on the Louisiana Purchase.

DUTY IN LONDON

Monroe was not so successful on his next diplomatic mission. In July 1803 Jefferson sent him to England. Relations between the two countries had been deteriorating. Monroe was concerned for his reception because of his well-known feelings toward France. However, the British government greeted him politely, if not warmly. Monroe's mission was to negotiate a treaty that would end trouble between the two countries over freedom of the seas. He was also sent to talk about the British **impressment** of American sailors. The Royal Navy in the early nineteenth century often stopped U.S. vessels on the high seas in search for British deserters. In the process, the British might capture naturalized American citizens who were on board. The United States wanted that practice to stop.

During the early 1800s, it was not uncommon for the British navy to stop and board U.S. ships and capture its seamen.

Great Britain did not want to compromise, perhaps because once more it was at war with France. So, Monroe left England and traveled to Spain to assist Minister Charles Pinckney in trying to obtain the Florida territory that Spain now owned. The United States wanted to buy it, or at least adjust the boundaries since so many Americans were moving into the area. The Spanish, however, were not interested in selling the land to the United States at the time.

Monroe was back in London again in 1805 with envoy William Pinckney in an attempt to get the British to agree to a treaty. In 1806 a treaty was drawn up that resolved some commercial conflicts between the two nations. However, it included nothing about impressments. Monroe thought it was the best deal possible under the circumstances, but Jefferson disagreed. He refused to give the treaty to Congress for a vote. James Madison, then secretary of state, also voiced his disapproval of the treaty.

A Bumpy Climb Back

Jefferson did not send Monroe on further diplomatic missions, so once again, he was out of a job. However, John Randolph of Roanoke, Virginia, urged him to become a candidate for the upcoming presidential election of 1808. Randolph, a prominent congressman from 1799 to 1829, disliked Jefferson. He believed that Jefferson and Madison were designing U.S. foreign policy to make sure that Madison would be the next president. Randolph urged Monroe to run. Monroe, himself hurt by Jefferson's and Madison's reactions to the treaty, agreed. As a result, Virginia came up with two electoral slates, one for Madison and one for Monroe. Randolph and Monroe need not have bothered; Madison won easily and became the fourth president of the United States.

To help establish his party's confidence in him, Monroe returned to the Virginia House of Delegates in April 1810. Later that year, when it seemed to Monroe that the Republican Party in

Virginia was in disarray, he decided to run for governor again. He was reelected on January 16, 1811, and used his diplomatic skills to bring harmony to the party.

Monroe's tenure as governor was brief, just three months. Through an **intermediary** he learned that Madison wanted him to become secretary of state.

MADISON'S CABINET

Madison's first secretary of state was Robert Smith, who was secretary of the navy under Jefferson. But Smith turned out to be a careless administrator and often loudly criticized the administration. When Madison looked for a replacement, he could find no one with as much experience in foreign affairs as Monroe. So, despite Monroe's problems in England and despite the strained friendship, Madison offered Monroe the position.

Monroe accepted and the two men put their previous difficulties behind them. This was a great career move for Monroe. The position of secretary of state is the nation's highest cabinet post.

This was a good time for Monroe but a dangerous time for the United States. Relations with Great Britain were getting worse. With no treaty outlawing impressments, the Royal Navy was still impressing U.S. seamen. There was also tension along the U.S.–Canadian border. The British were supplying arms to Shawnee leader Tecumseh in hopes of stopping the Americans from entering western territory. On November 7, 1811, the Battle of Tippecanoe was fought between U.S. forces led by Governor William Henry Harrison of the Indiana Territory and Tecumseh's men. After that, many congressmen began to cry for war.

At the Battle of Tippecanoe, Native Americans battled American troops to protect and keep their land that they had lived on for thousands of years.

THE WAR OF 1812

Finally, on June 1, 1812, Madison sent a war message to Congress. War was declared on June 18. Monroe immediately asked for an assignment in the military, but Madison needed him in the government. The United States was not prepared for a war with Great Britain. When the Americans quickly lost some early battles, Madison decided to replace William Eustis, his secretary of

TIPPECANOE AND TYLER, TOO!

The Battle of Tippecanoe took place at the Native-American capital on the Tippecanoe River near Lafayette, Indiana. It was led by Tenskwatawa, brother of Shawnee chief Tecumseh. Major General William Henry Harrison repelled the Shawnee and burned their village. Both sides suffered about equal losses, but the United States claimed victory.

When Harrison ran for president in 1840, he used the slogan "Tippecanoe and Tyler, too!" John Tyler was his vice president. At his inauguration, Harrison stood in the cold March wind and gave a speech lasting almost two hours. He developed pneumonia and died after just one month in office. Tyler became the nation's tenth president.

war. He asked Monroe to fill the post, which he did for ten weeks until John Armstrong was appointed. He was a former senator, minister to France, and brigadier general.

Against the British superior odds at sea, the United States managed to win some naval battles. The most famous took place on August 19, 1812, off the coast of Halifax, Nova Scotia. The USS *Constitution* sighted the *Guerriére*, a frigate of the Royal Navy. For a time the two ships fired at each other with little damage. But on the evening of August 19, they drew close and the *Constitution* began to batter the British ship. Finally, the *Guerriére*'s tall mast fell over, tangling both ships. Many were killed or

The most well-known naval battle of the War of 1812 took place between the USS Constitution *and the* HMS Guerriére.

wounded. The British captain surrendered at about 7:00 P.M. This first victory at sea made the U.S. Navy feel it could fight the mighty British fleet.

But on land, victories were scarce for the Americans in the War of 1812. Monroe thought that Armstrong was a poor war secretary, so Monroe continued to give military advice to the president. One of the things he advised was better protection for the nation's capital. His advice was not taken. On August 24, 1814, British troops entered Washington, D.C., and burned the city. When the British left Washington, Congress returned and

THE WHITE HOUSE BURNS

President Madison did not take Monroe's advice about extra protection for Washington, D.C., and the White House. In early August Madison learned that about four thousand British sailors had entered Chesapeake Bay and threatened the capital. U.S. soldiers were stationed on the White House lawn to protect the president. On the morning of August 24, while Madison was away, he learned that British troops were nearing the White House. Madison sent word to his wife, Dolley, the First Lady, to leave immediately.

Dolley Madison did not panic. She took the time to gather important papers and save a new portrait of George Washington (it hangs in the White House today). The British almost completely destroyed the White House. However, before doing so, they ate the supper that had been planned for the president's return.

(continued)

Many members of Congress wanted to rebuild the White House in another city or location, but Madison refused. He said the building should be restored on its original site. It would not be completed until the term of the next president, James Monroe.

Armstrong resigned. Monroe was once again acting secretary of war. As such he helped with plans to defend the city of Baltimore. The United States also had sea victories on the Great Lakes.

Monroe also helped to plan the defense of the city of Baltimore when the British attacked Fort McHenry on September 13. Watching the bombardment was a thirty-five-year-old lawyer and poet named Francis Scott Key. He was so inspired by the fierce battle that he wrote a poem called "The Star Spangled Banner." (In 1931 it became the national anthem of the United States.)

The last battle of the War of 1812 actually took place after the war was over. The peace treaty was signed on December 24, 1814. However, the news did not reach the United States in time to stop the fight on January 8, 1815. This was the famous Battle of New Orleans, when General Andrew Jackson sent some 7,000 troops—militiamen and volunteers—against about 7,500 British soldiers. The Americans had erected a defense of cotton bales that was so effective, the battle lasted only half an hour. The British withdrew after suffering more than two thousand casualties against only seventy-one for the Americans. The Battle of New Orleans made Jackson a hero; he would eventually become the seventh president of the United States.

Word of the peace treaty did not reach General Andrew Jackson in time as his troops proved victorious over the British in the Battle of New Orleans in early January 1815.

Monroe's conduct as secretaries of state and war had also done much to make him presidential material. The young nation survived the war. Americans began to feel better about the future, and the election of 1816 was just around the corner.

THE ERA OF GOOD FEELINGS

Four

The end of the War of 1812 and Monroe's participation in it put him in good standing for the presidency. Not as intellectual or popular as Jefferson or Madison, he was well known, well liked, and well respected. Even so, he had a problem—he was from Virginia. So were Washington, Jefferson, and Madison. When those men became president, they all gave important jobs in the government to other Virginians. Many people in both parties were starting to grumble about Virginians running the country. They wanted a change. But Monroe was part of the so-called Virginia dynasty.

The loudest anti-Virginia voices came from the powerful New York Republicans. They were determined to destroy the Virginia dynasty. But they were divided. Some wanted their own governor, Daniel D. Tompkins, who was little known outside the state. A bigger Republican threat came from William Crawford. He had been Madison's secretary of the treasury and was from Georgia. Crawford was very popular in the South and West.

On March 16 the Republicans gathered for a **caucus** to vote for a presidential candidate. Monroe's popularity with state leaders won the day. He received sixty-five votes to Crawford's fifty-four. The election itself was an easy victory. Monroe's opponent was Senator Rufus King of New York, a Federalist. But the Federalists, who had elected Washington and Adams, were no longer popular with the public. Neither Monroe nor

King even campaigned on their own behalf. Monroe carried all but three states, 183 electoral votes to 34 for King.

THE CABINET

Before inauguration day, Monroe named his cabinet. It turned out to be the best group of officials since George Washington's administration. Monroe's most important choice was secretary of state. He was determined to have peace and harmony in his administration. With the recent hostility toward Virginians, he was not

This emblem from a 1816 presidential campaign poster supports James Monroe against senator Rufus King.

going to appoint a southerner to the post that was so close to the presidency. Instead, Monroe chose John Quincy Adams of Massachusetts. Son of the second president, John Quincy, who was a Republican unlike his father, was well qualified and experienced. He had served as minister to the Netherlands (1794–1797), Prussia (1797–1801), and Russia (1809–1815); as U.S. Minister to Great Britain (1815–1816); and had been a U.S. senator (1803–1808). Monroe and Adams got along well. The new secretary of state was unequaled in his ability to present his views with clarity and persuasiveness.

Among the other members of Monroe's first cabinet were his former rival Crawford as secretary of the treasury and the youngest member, John C. Calhoun, as war secretary. One of

As president, one of James Monroe's first appointments was John Quincy Adams (above) as secretary of state.

the nation's leading lawyers, William Wirt, was named attorney general. All of these people, with the exception of Benjamin W. Crowninshield as secretary of the navy, remained with Monroe for his entire eight years in office. The navy secretary resigned in 1818 after Monroe scolded him for making mistakes in arranging a presidential inspection tour of military forts. The least-known member of Monroe's administration was his vice president, Daniel Tompkins. The current New York governor, he was chosen mainly to appease New York Republicans.

INAUGURATION DAY

Fifty-eight-year-old James Monroe took the oath of office on March 4, 1817, in the unusually mild outdoors of Washington, D.C. At the last minute, the location of the ceremony was changed. It had been set to take place in the rooms where the House of Representatives was meeting until the rebuilding of the burned-out Capitol was finished. The *National Intelligencer* reported that the change was made because the temporary building might collapse with so many people inside. Some eight thousand people came to the ceremony, the largest crowd of any presidential inauguration at that time.

James Monroe took the oath of office on March 4, 1817.

But the real reason for the outdoor ceremony was, according to reports, Henry Clay of Kentucky, Speaker of the House. He was highly annoyed because he was not appointed secretary of state. When the Senate wanted to move its red velvet chairs over to the House to sit on during the ceremony, Clay said no. And he would not budge. So, Monroe became the first president to take the oath of office outside. Clay did not attend the ceremony.

This portrait of James Monroe was painted by John Vanderlyn in 1816, around the time that Monroe was voted into office.

When Monroe became president, there were nineteen states in the Union and about 9 million people in the country. Half of them lived in the eastern seaboard states. Agriculture was still the main work of the land, but manufacturing was growing rapidly. The largest state in terms of population was Virginia and the largest populated city was Philadelphia.

Monroe was not a strong speaker, but in his inaugural speech he spoke of his sense of responsibility toward the office of the president: "From a just responsibility I will never shrink, calculating with confidence that in my best efforts to promote the public welfare my motives will always be duly appreciated and my conduct be viewed with that candor and indulgence which I have experienced in other stations." He also spoke of the departing president: "I shall be pardoned for expressing my earnest wishes that he may long enjoy in his retirement the affections of a grateful country." And he spoke of war: "War became at length inevitable, and the result has shown that our Government is equal to that, the greatest of trials, under the most unfavorable circumstances. Of the virtue of the people and of the heroic exploits of the Army, the Navy, and the militia I need not speak."

Monroe also talked about the health of the country and the need for more roads and canals. The United States was expanding west, and its growth was very important to Monroe. He called for a stronger military. Although the navy had performed well against the British, Monroe knew that the young country was still very weak. Danger could come from foreign countries unless the United States could defend itself.

A DIGNIFIED WHITE HOUSE

When Monroe was elected, Washington society could hardly wait for repairs to the White House to be completed. Dolley Madison, the previous First Lady, had given such wonderful parties, but society was in for a shock when James and Elizabeth Monroe moved in. The beautiful First Lady was not only far more reserved than Dolley Madison, she was also in poor health. Customs changed immediately. Elizabeth Monroe refused to answer every and all invitations, as previous first ladies had done. No longer were visitors allowed just to "drop in." Because of her health, the First Lady often sent daughter Eliza to teas or dinners in her place. Official dinners were formal. They were elegant, but some guests complained that the Monroes were stingy about the amount of food they served. They also said the dining table was so wide that no one could hear what the person on the other side was saying. The White House became a formal place of invitation-only events and gracious dining, much as it is today.

The Good Feelings Tour

Before Monroe got down to the business of being president, he and his wife toured the northern states. The tour was billed as a trip to inspect forts and shipyards. But the president really hoped it would help to make the nation feel unified. As it turned out, this was the trip that named his administration the Era of Good Feelings. By steamboat and carriage, on horseback and on foot, the Monroes traveled as far west as Detroit and as far north as Maine.

Monroe had been somewhat worried about his reception in New England. He had lost Massachusetts and Connecticut in the election. But his fears soon subsided. Everywhere the Monroes stopped, bands played and people came out to wave and cheer.

At each stop Monroe gave a speech. He wanted all Americans to feel as one. He wanted them all to work together to build a stronger country.

Monroe's good feelings tour lasted about sixteen weeks. He was back in Washington in September 1817 and in the newly finished White House soon after that. The damage from the War of 1812 was finally repaired.

The Florida Problem

Besides concern over the nation's strength, Monroe was worried about Florida. For a number of years the United States had been trying to buy the Florida territory from Spain. One of the reasons was simply that America wanted to expand its territory. But the need for Florida had now grown more urgent. Hostile Seminole

Native Americans—who had already lost land to the Americans—and escaped slaves were making raids from Florida into Georgia. They killed the residents and stole their cattle. It became clear to Monroe that Spain would not, or could not, do anything about the problem.

So, Monroe gave Andrew Jackson, a hero of the Battle of New Orleans, a rather general order. He was to cross over into Florida territory and push the raiders back. It was a poor decision on Monroe's part. General Jackson was a brave fighter, but he had a violent temper and he disliked Native Americans. Also, he most always thought he was right. In this case he went beyond Monroe's rather vague order. He crossed the order and took a Spanish military outpost. Then, he executed two British subjects whom he charged with inciting the Seminoles. Next, he attacked the Seminoles themselves and destroyed their villages. Within weeks he had thrown out the Spanish governor and replaced him with an American.

The U.S. public thought Jackson was a hero for his swift action, but it was an embarrassment for the administration. The House of Representatives opened a debate on Jackson's conduct, but a resolution to censure him was defeated.

Strangely enough, Jackson's hasty, unlawful actions produced the results that Monroe wanted. Spain decided that perhaps its possession of Florida was not such a good idea. Secretary of State Adams pointed out that the Spanish did not seem to be able to defend the territory anyway.

Bargaining went on for months. Finally, in 1819, Spain ceded the Florida territory to the United States. Also, as part of the Adams-Onís (the Spanish minister) Treaty, the Rocky Mountains

On the orders of President Monroe, General Andrew Jackson and his troops crossed into the Florida territory to gain it back from Spain.

became the western boundary of the Louisiana Territory. Spain also gave up claims to Oregon. However, Spain did keep all of modern Texas. This was a rather remarkable treaty. The United States paid only $5 million worth of claims that Americans held against the Spanish government. For that, the nation now extended to the Rocky Mountains. In addition, a window was open to the Pacific Ocean because the United States held the Oregon territory with Great Britain.

WEDDING IN THE WHITE HOUSE

In 1820 Monroe's second daughter, Maria, became the first person to be married in the White House. At the age of seventeen, she wed Samuel L. Gouverneur, aide to the president. Washington society was shocked again because the wedding was a private ceremony with only family and close friends attending. All the papers could report was that the bridal party consisted of seven bridesmaids and seven groomsmen.

Unlike her mother and older sister, Maria was said to be a friendly young girl. But Washington saw little of her. After her marriage, the couple lived in New York City and rarely visited the White House.

THE PANIC OF 1819

Along with trouble in Florida, Monroe had to worry about money, but this time it was the country's money. The first depression hit the nation in 1819. The first Bank of the United States was established by Alexander Hamilton in 1791. It lasted until 1811. The second Bank of the United States was set up in 1816, but it was badly managed. That helped to bring on the panic and depression of 1819, which lasted about three years.

William Crawford, secretary of the treasury, helped to ease the pain of the depression. Many Americans were about to lose their land because they could not keep up the loan payments. Crawford's plan allowed them to delay payment on the debt.

THE MISSOURI COMPROMISE

In 1820 President Monroe faced an issue that divided the nation and threatened the government. It concerned slavery.

The problem began quietly enough in 1818. Congress was considering a request for statehood from the territory of Missouri. At that time, there were twenty-two states in the Union; eleven were slave states and eleven were free states. This balance helped to keep the slavery issue from splitting the nation. But trouble began in 1819 when James Tallmadge, congressman from New York, wanted to add something to the Missouri statehood bill. His amendment said that no more slaves could be brought into the state. It also said that slaves already in Missouri would be freed when they reached the age of twenty-five.

Congress got into an angry and ugly debate over slavery. By the time it adjourned, the question of Missouri's statehood had not been settled. But when Congress met again in December, there was a new issue. The territory of Maine asked for admission as a free state.

Senator Henry Clay led Congress to a compromise. Maine would be admitted as a free state. Missouri would be admitted with no restrictions on slavery. However, except for Missouri, slavery would be banned in the country north of latitude 36'30". This is the Missouri Compromise.

Monroe stayed in the background of this fight over slavery. Part of the reason was that he was a slaveholder himself. He was also a southerner. When the bill came to his desk in March 1820, he thought about a veto. He even thought that the bill might be unconstitutional because it did not allow states to decide whether they wished to be slave or free. But most of all

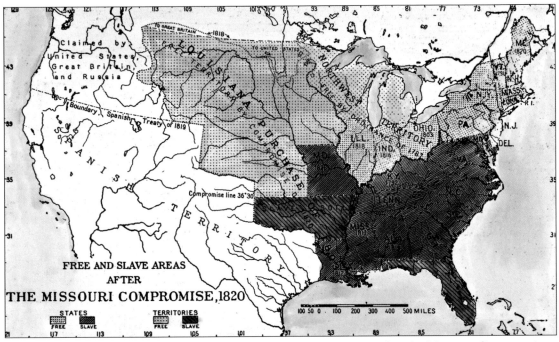

FREE AND SLAVE AREAS
AFTER
THE MISSOURI COMPROMISE, 1820

A map of the United States in 1820 illustrates free and slave states after the Missouri Compromise.

he worried about what might happen if the Missouri Compromise was not signed into law. Would the country erupt into civil war? Monroe could not take that chance, and so he signed the bill.

As Monroe's first term drew to a close, he could look back with some confidence. The United States had survived its first economic depression. It had also grown with the addition of the Florida territory. Monroe was relieved that the Missouri-Maine issue had been solved—at least for now. But the president and others in Congress realized the problem was only delayed for a while. It would take another forty years before slavery in the United States came to its end in civil war.

THE MONROE DOCTRINE

*J*ames Monroe was a dedicated and competent president. But any of his successes or failures are overshadowed by the doctrine that bears his name. The Monroe Doctrine, enacted during his second term, concerns U.S. policy toward other nations.

THE SECOND TERM BEGINS

Monroe ran unopposed for his second term. No one in government at the time had the political and public following to beat him. Even so, Monroe did not get all the electoral votes. When the presidential electors cast their ballots, William Plumer of New Hampshire voted for John Quincy Adams. Monroe won the election with 231 electoral votes to 1. According to the popular tale, Plumer cast his negative vote to keep Washington as the only unanimous president. Plumer himself said that he did not like Monroe's response to the panic of 1819.

As Monroe began his second term, some of that era of good feelings was fading. A lot of bitterness existed because of the fight over Missouri. There was growing uneasiness over the question of slavery. And since Monroe was the only candidate in the presidential race, there was little enthusiasm for the election itself, and voting was light. Few objected to Monroe, although many objected to Tompkins running again as vice president.

Nevertheless, as he began his second term, Monroe was feeling good about the country. The Florida problem had been settled.

James Monroe began his second term as president on the coattails of the Era of Good Feelings.

The climate surrounding the admission of Missouri into the Union was still uneasy, but it became a state on August 10, 1821.

THE MONROE DOCTRINE

During his seventh year in office, on December 2, 1823, Monroe gave his annual message to the U.S. Congress. In his speech, Monroe said he was concerned that both Spain and Russia were interested in establishing new colonies in the Western Hemisphere. Monroe declared:

As a principle in which the rights and interests of the United States are involved, that the American continents, by the free and independent condition which they have assumed and maintain, are henceforth not to be considered as subjects for future colonization by any European powers.

A DREAM GONE WRONG

James Monroe is the only U.S. president who has the capital of a foreign country named after him. It is Monrovia, Liberia, in western Africa, and it is Africa's oldest republic. The American Colonization Society (ACS) was founded in 1817. Monroe was a member, even though he was a slaveholder. Like other members of the ACS, he tried to think of how to end slavery. One idea was to free the slaves, a few at a time, and return them to Africa. Land was bought on the African continent, and in the early 1820s the colony of Liberia was founded. Its capital was Monrovia (below), named after the president.

(continued)

Even though Monroe and others had good intentions, the experiment did not work. It was hard for American slaves to adjust to a new life in Africa. Most of them were born in America and had never seen Africa.

The struggles that began the new republic still go on. In 2003 the United Nations was called in to restore peace in the middle of a bitter civil war. In 2005 Ellen Johnson-Sirleaf won a runoff election for president.

Monroe was telling the Congress, and the world, that the Western Hemisphere would stay as it was. No European power, or anyone else, was going to start new colonies in North or South America. He also said that the United States would look on inference by foreign powers as a hostile act; in other words, war.

That policy statement to Congress is called the Monroe Doctrine. Those are the words by which the presidency of James Monroe is remembered. It became the basis of U.S. foreign policy. Yet, they are not Monroe's words. The Monroe Doctrine was mostly written by Secretary of State John Quincy Adams, who would become the next U.S. president.

No matter who wrote it, the Monroe Doctrine was a bold challenge. It did not, however, make a great impact on the nations of Europe. France had already discarded plans to reclaim Latin America. The czar of Russia had already taken back his threat to invade Alaskan waters. But if they had wanted to add colonies in the Western Hemisphere, who would stop them? The United States was far from a world power in 1823. Overall, the leaders

An early twentieth-century political cartoon satirizes the Monroe Doctrine.

of Europe regarded the president's declaration as merely arrogant words with little else to back them up.

The House chamber was crowded on the day of the president's address. It is doubtful that the audience thought much of it because it is doubtful that they heard much of it. Monroe spoke in a very low voice. There was no such thing as crowd control, and the noise from the spectators was quite loud. In addition, the large room caused a dreadful echo, so a speaker's voice was not clear. After the speech, the marine band played "Yankee Doodle" and the president went home.

THE DOCTRINE LIVES

President James Polk brought up the Monroe Doctrine in his first annual message to Congress in 1845. There was talk at the time about extending the United States "from the Atlantic to the Pacific." Polk was anxious to do it before England or France could interfere. So, he told the world in his message that the people of "this continent alone have the right to decide their own destiny." That is known as the Polk corollary to the Monroe Doctrine.

President Grover Cleveland dealt with violations of the Monroe Doctrine during his first term (1885–89). The United States had a treaty to establish a naval base on the Pacific island of Samoa. When Germany tried to install a government there, Cleveland sent in warships. He also interfered with the boundary dispute between Venezuela and Great Britain over British Guiana.

In 1905 President Theodore Roosevelt added the Roosevelt Corollary to the doctrine. He said that if a Latin-American country was guilty of chronic or obvious wrongdoing, it was right for the United States to interfere. This was part of what came to be known as the president's Big Stick Diplomacy. He had once said, "Speak softly and carry a big stick; you will go far." Until the administration of Franklin D. Roosevelt, the United States frequently interfered in Latin America. Through Roosevelt's Good Neighbor Policy, the United States renounced its right to interfere in the internal affairs of other American nations.

John Quincy Adams had been working on the words that became the Monroe Doctrine for some time. Many of the newly independent nations in Central and South America were former Spanish colonies. As the new nations prospered, Great Britain was afraid that Spain would want to recolonize them. That would close their markets to Britain. At one point, George Canning, the British foreign minister, suggested to Monroe that the United States and Great Britain issue a declaration together that forbid colonization. Monroe agreed at first, as did former president Jefferson. But John Quincy argued that such a declaration should come from the United States alone. Monroe changed his mind. The Monroe Doctrine contains the thoughts and words of Adams. But Monroe decided it was a policy that he could support and he chose to announce it in his message to Congress. Therefore, it is his most lasting contribution to his presidency.

For more than a quarter century after the Monroe Doctrine was announced, America's foreign policy dealt mainly with the Western Hemisphere. From the administration of Thomas Jefferson on, there was a growing belief that the United States must expand westward. He believed, as did John Quincy Adams, that one day the country would extend from coast to coast. The Monroe Doctrine helped to ensure that the country would be free to do so.

THE HANDS-ON PRESIDENT

Monroe was very much a hands-on president. Although the country was growing rapidly, it was still small enough so that he had direct contact with the heads of different government departments. Monroe tried to concern himself especially with issues that promoted the growth of the country. Sometimes he ran into opposition with Congress. One such issue was the so-called Cumberland Road.

The Cumberland Road is the first national highway in the United States. It was built from 1811 to about 1837 from Cumberland, Maryland, to Vandalia, Illinois. It is now part of U.S. Route 40. In Monroe's second term, Congress passed a law to repair the road by building gates and collecting tolls.

Monroe surprised everyone by vetoing the bill. He had always supported western expansion and his act angered the westerners. Actually, Monroe really was in support of expansion,

During Monroe's second term, he passed a bill that allocated $30,000 toward the building and upkeep of the Cumberland Road.

but he felt that collecting tolls was not the job of the federal government. After much debate, in 1824 Congress passed a bill allocating $30,000 for road building and repairs. Monroe signed it.

The Last Year

Monroe's last year in office was not his happiest. Early in his second term, he had said he would not seek another four years. (The two-term limit did not take effect until Amendment XXII was ratified in 1951.) That left the election of 1824 wide open. Many people wanted the job, including three in Monroe's own cabinet. They were John Quincy Adams, secretary of state; John C. Calhoun, secretary of war; and William Crawford, secretary of the treasury. Two other powerful government figures were also in the running: Speaker of the House Henry Clay and military hero Andrew Jackson.

Monroe liked harmony and unity in government. There was little of either one during his last year as president. Monroe also disliked fighting. There was plenty of that. The three contenders were constantly fighting with each other. Each tried to make himself look good for the upcoming election.

The president tried to stay apart from all the bickering in his cabinet. Nor did he voice any approval for one candidate over the other. But it was obvious that the Era of Good Feelings was gone. There was so much ill will tossed about that Monroe's own policies were often denounced, which hurt him deeply.

The run for the presidency also cost Monroe an important treaty. Richard Rush, U.S. minister in London, had confirmed a pact with the British to stop the international slave trade. This involved the transport of slaves across the Atlantic. The treaty said that the slave trade was piracy. Therefore, ships could be searched.

TWO OLD FRIENDS

A bright spot in Monroe's last year in office was the arrival of his old friend Marquis de Lafayette (left). It also took attention away from the upcoming election. Lafayette returned to France in 1782 after his service in the American Revolution. He had last visited the United States in 1784.

Americans greeted Lafayette with great warmth when he arrived in New York Harbor on August 15. Monroe greeted him in Washington as Lafayette was on his way to Yorktown to celebrate the British surrender. Lafayette's last public appearance was as the guest of honor for a dinner at the University of Virginia. Jefferson and Madison attended, but Monroe had to return to Washington because Congress was convening.

At his last annual message to Congress, Monroe spoke warmly of Lafayette. He asked that the nation show gratitude for his longtime friend. He did not say that Lafayette was practically without funds. However, that was well known. Congress appropriated $200,000 and a township of land to Lafayette.

Monroe submitted the treaty to the Senate in April 1824. The House had already approved resolutions that said the slave trade was piracy. But the Senate was too caught up in the election. Senators could only agree on a treaty that said the right to search ships was limited to the coast of Africa. Great Britain rejected that, and the treaty was lost.

NATIVE-AMERICAN AFFAIRS

During his years in office, Monroe was caught up in issues that involved Native Americans. On this subject he was more forward thinking than most. He stated in his 1817 message to Congress that Native Americans must be given their own lands. Monroe felt that this would force them to give up their nomadic lifestyles and settle down in one place. But to most Americans, that meant they would eventually become part of American communities. Neither Congress nor the American people were ready for that.

Under great pressure from Georgia, Monroe requested money from Congress for the purchase of Cherokee land in that state in 1820. Two years later Congress offered $30,000. The Cherokee refused. The governor of Georgia vowed to remove them by force. (That eventually happened during the fall and winter of 1838–1839 under President Andrew Jackson. The Cherokee were forced westward in what became known as the Trail of Tears.)

Just before he left office, Monroe had apparently given up on his Native-American policy. He reported to Congress that natives should be removed west of the Mississippi River. He stated that it seemed impossible to take the Native Americans

In 1838 the Cherokee were forced off their land and made to move west to new territory.

into the American system in such large masses. He also said that if U.S. policy did not change, the extermination of the Native American was certain. No action was taken.

At the time of Monroe's last annual message to Congress, in December 1824, rumor pointed to a presidential race between Adams and Jackson. On February 9, 1825, the votes were counted. John Quincy Adams became the sixth president of the United States.

James Monroe prepared to go home to Virginia. His wife was gravely ill and it was feared she would die. And so, after eight years in the White House, the last president of the American Revolution left the political scene. He was sixty-six years old.

MONROE GOES HOME *Six*

$\mathcal{A}$ chapter closed when James Monroe left the White House in 1825. The Era of Good Feelings ended and the American Revolution took its place in the nation's history. A new era began. The old-fashioned president with the knee breeches and kindly manner left the running of the country to younger people. Monroe returned to his beloved Virginia.

BACK TO OAK HILL

James Monroe was proud of his record as president, even though the country was not feeling as good about itself when he left as when he had started. Yet, he felt he had done his best, and most agreed with him. Even so, Monroe was relieved to return to the family estate, Oak Hill, in Loudon County. He hoped that a long stay in the peaceful Virginian countryside would help to restore his wife's health. It did to some extent. Monroe and his wife lived at Oak Hill until her death in 1830.

Monroe worked hard at Oak Hill after his retirement. He raised sheep and grew wheat, rye, and other grains. Helping him keep the farm at that time were some twenty slaves. In earlier years there had been as many as seventy. He had been advised to sell the slaves to help him get out of debt, but Monroe was afraid that the families would be separated.

Because of Elizabeth Monroe's illness, daughter Eliza and her husband lived at Oak Hill much of the time. Monroe's granddaughter, Hortensia, grew up there until she married and moved to Baltimore. In 1828 Elizabeth felt well enough for a trip to New York

THE PRESIDENT'S HOME

Monroe's estate, called Oak Hill, was built between 1820 and 1823. He had inherited the land from an uncle in 1808. Both Thomas Jefferson and James Hoban, architect of the White House, helped to design it. During his second term, Monroe spent as much time as he could at Oak Hill, which is about 30 miles from Washington, D.C. He often made the trip on horseback. Monroe lived there until 1830, the year before he died.

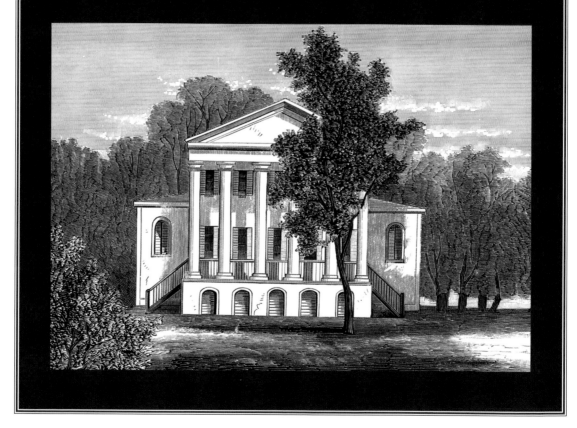

Oak Hill is named for the trees that he planted on the property, one for each state in the Union during his lifetime.

After Monroe's death, the estate was sold. It was originally a two-story building with small one-room wings on either side. In 1923 the wings were enlarged to two full stories. Oak Hill is still a private residence and is not open to the public.

to visit daughter Maria and her family. That was the first time Monroe saw his younger daughter since he left the White House. The Monroes were especially concerned about Maria's eldest child, James, who was born deaf and unable to speak. They also had two other grandchildren, Elizabeth and Samuel.

In October 1829 Monroe returned to public office one last time. He was the presiding officer at the Virginia Constitutional Convention held in Richmond. Other elder statesmen were also present, such as John Marshall, John Randolph of Roanoke, and Governor William Branch Giles. Monroe's health was in question since he was suffering the effects of a fall from his horse the previous year. But it was decided that his daughter Eliza would go with him to the convention. Even so, it was obvious that the former president's health was failing. Monroe attended the sessions for two months before he had to resign. When the subject of slavery was raised, he said he favored ultimate emancipation and deportation of blacks.

In his latter years, Monroe returned to political life, only to resign after two short months of service due to poor health.

In September 1830, after many years of ill health, Elizabeth Monroe died at Oak Hill. The president was deeply unhappy. Theirs had been a long and happy marriage.

Monroe was plagued by money problems during his retirement years. He sold land that he owned in Virginia and Kentucky, but most of all he relied on payment from Congress. Shortly before he left office, Monroe sent a message to Congress concerning his finances. He asked for consideration of his years abroad as a diplomat. Although he had been paid the usual diplomatic fees, he had not been able to take charge of his plantation and lands at home. This was not an unusual complaint from U.S. diplomats at the time. The young government was noted for being stingy with its payments to those who served abroad. Their salaries were rarely adequate to keep them in the style that was expected in European capitals.

After a long and thorough accounting, Monroe requested some $53,000 for his past services. Congress considered his plea for a long time. Finally, in 1831, Monroe was given slightly less than $30,000.

The Last Years

Monroe was never the same after his wife's death. In fact, his health grew so poor that his daughters decided he could no longer live at Oak Hill. He and Eliza, whose husband died shortly before her mother, went to New York to live with Maria and her family. By the end of the year, Monroe was too ill to leave his room. He died there July 4, at three o'clock in the afternoon. He was seventy-three years old.

An elaborate funeral procession filled the streets of New York. President Andrew Jackson honored the day with a naval

James Monroe lied in state at New York's City Hall.

salute. Church bells rang all over the country. At a service in Boston, John Quincy Adams spoke of Monroe's long and dedicated service to his nation. The country seemed to see his death as the end of the revolutionary generation. Monroe was buried in New York City, but in 1858 his body was returned to Virginia and reburied in a cemetery in Richmond.

The fifth president of the United States died in 1831. In a strange coincidence of history, Presidents John Adams and Thomas Jefferson had both died on July 4, 1826. Five years later, James Monroe became the third U.S. president to die on the Fourth of July, the birthday of the nation.

THE LEGACY OF JAMES MONROE

When James Monroe left the White House, there was no longer an era of good feelings. He had contributed to that change partly because he did not want to become involved in the bitter fight for the presidency among his cabinet members. But changes were also occurring in the country that had little to do with Monroe's leadership and his legacy.

Slave states and free states were becoming more and more opposed to each other. The fight over slavery in the United States was becoming more violent and bitter. The national economy had grown under Monroe, but there were signs that prosperity was about to end.

Monroe suffered defeats in his long career, such as his diplomatic service in France and his trouble with Jackson in Florida. But he could also take pride in his part of the Louisiana Purchase and the growth of the nation to the Pacific. During his years before and during his presidency, the economic and physical growth of the United States had been one of Monroe's most pressing concerns.

As president, Monroe was a well-liked, familiar figure around Washington. He had grown into a tall-standing, gray-haired man with a face that was deeply lined. He was not a person who aroused great emotion, but he did earn great respect for his long years of devotion to his country.

James Monroe was the last of the Virginia dynasty. His administration ended an era that had been led by the South. In one sense, his eight years in office ended as they had begun, with the warm wishes of the nation. When he left office, Monroe received many thanks from state governments and individual leaders for his devoted service. Not everyone agreed with James Monroe or his policies, but they never doubted his dedication to his country.

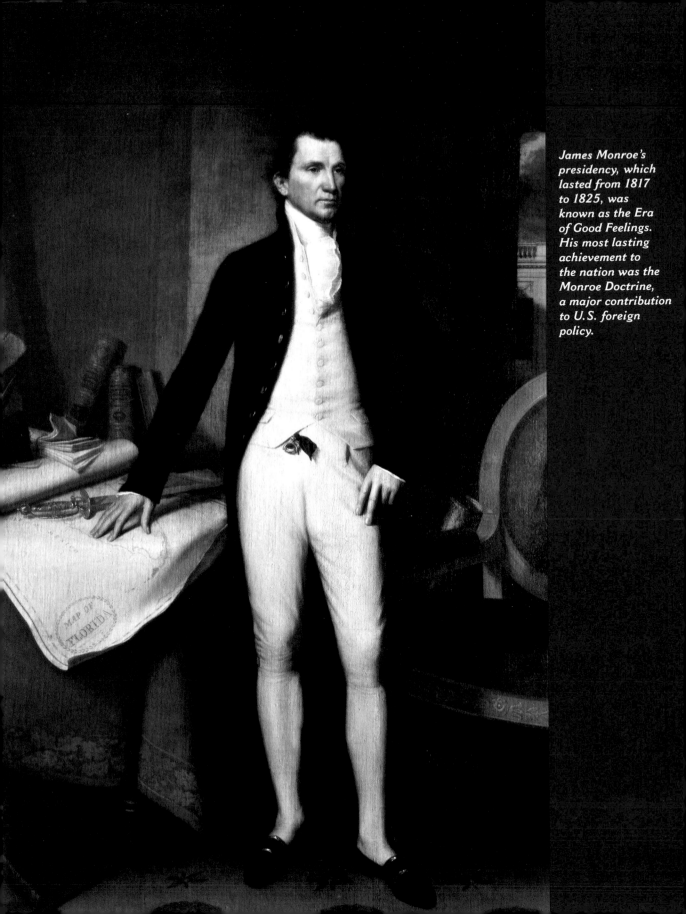

James Monroe's presidency, which lasted from 1817 to 1825, was known as the Era of Good Feelings. His most lasting achievement to the nation was the Monroe Doctrine, a major contribution to U.S. foreign policy.

TIMELINE

1758
Born in Westmoreland County, Virginia, April 28

1774
Enters College of William and Mary

1776
Joins Third Virginia Regiment of Foot

1780
Begins study of law with Thomas Jefferson in Richmond

1782
Joins Virginia House of Delegates

1783
Becomes a member of the Continental Congress

1786
Passes the bar, opens law practice in Fredericksburg; marries Elizabeth Kortright

1790
Is elected to U.S. Senate

1750

1794
Is appointed minister to France by George Washington

1799
Becomes governor of Virginia

1810
Joins Virginia House of Delegates

1811
Becomes governor again for three months; becomes James Madison's secretary of state

1816
Becomes fifth president of the United States

1823
Delivers Monroe Doctrine speech during second term

1825
Retires to Virginia

1831
Dies July 4 in New York City

1840

GLOSSARY

Anti-Federalist those who opposed a central government

caucus closed meeting of party members to select candidates or decide on a policy

commission a certificate that gives military rank and authority

Continental Congress body of delegates who acted for the people of the colonies that later became the United States

corollary something that naturally follows something else, such as an addition to a proposal or law

damages compensation in excess of actual damage

delegate representative at a convention or conference; one who speaks for others

envoy someone who represents one government to another

federalist those who favored a strong federal government

impressment seizing people for public service

intermediary someone who speaks for someone else

landed gentry landowners who are well thought of in society

ratification formal approval, such as of a constitution

repeal to remove a law

FURTHER INFORMATION

BOOKS

Hossell, Karen Price. *The Declaration of Independence*. Chicago:

Heinemann, 2004.

Levy, Debby. *James Monroe*. San Diego: Lerner, 2004.

Nardo, Don. *The American Revolution*. San Diego: Gale, 2003.

Santella, Andrew. *James Monroe*. Danbury, CT: Children's Press, 2003.

WEB SITES

American Presidents

www.americanpresidents.org/presidents/president.asp?PresidentNumber=5
This site includes fast facts on the life of President James Monroe.

American Revolution

www.nps.gov/revwar
An American Revolution Web site of the National Park Service where
the people, places, and events of the Revolutionary War can be explored.

James Monroe

www.monroefoundation.org
This site preserves the life of James Monroe and his legacy.

BIBLIOGRAPHY

American Heritage, eds. *The American Heritage Book of the Presidents and Famous Americans*. New York: Dell, 1967.

Ammon, Harry. *James Monroe: The Quest for National Identity*. Charlottesville: University of Virginia Press, 1990.

Burke's Presidential Families of the United States of America. London: Burke's Peerage, 1975.

Cunningham, Noble E. Jr. *The Presidency of James Monroe*. Lawrence: University of Kansas Press, 1996.

Degregorio, William. *The Complete Book of the U.S. Presidents*. New York: Barricade, 1993.

Diller, Daniel C., and Stephen L. Robertson. *The Presidents, First Ladies, and Vice Presidents: White House Biographies, 1789–2001*. Washington, D.C.: CQ Press, 2001.

Gruver, Rebecca Brooks. *An American History*, Volume 1 to 1877. Reading, MA: Addison-Wesley, 1972.

Kane, Joseph Nathan, Janet Podell, and Steven Anzovin. *Facts About the Presidents*. New York: Wilson, 2001.

Klapthor, Margaret Brown. *The First Ladies*. Washington, D.C.: White House Historical Association, 1981.

Magill, Frank N., John L. Loos, and Tracy Irons-Georges. *The American Presidents*. Pasadena, CA: Salem, 2000.

Styron, Arthur. *The Last of the Cocked Hats: James Monroe & the Virginia Dynasty*. Norman: University of Oklahoma Press, 1945.

Taylor, Tim. *The Book of Presidents*. New York: Arno, 1972.

Whitney, David C. *The American Presidents*, 8th ed. Pleasantville, NY: Reader's Digest, 1996.

PERIODICALS

Burstein, Andrew. "Jefferson's Madison versus Jefferson's Monroe," *Presidential Studies Quarterly* 28, no, 2 (Spring 1998).

Harriss, Joseph. "Westward Ho!" *Smithsonian* 34, no. 1 (April 2003).

Holmes, David L. "The Religion of James Monroe," *Virgina Quarterly Review* 79, no. 4 (Autumn 2003).

Johnson, Monroe. "James Monroe, Soldier," *William and Mary College Quarterly Historical Magazine* 9, no. 2 (April 1929).

Rutland, Robert Allen. "Madison vs. Monroe: The Final Struggle for a Bill of Rights," *Humanties* 12, no. 6 (Nov./Dec. 1991).

Scherr, Arthur. "The Confidence of His Country: James Monroe on Impeachement," *Midwest Quarterly* 44, no. 1 (Autumn 2002).

Turner, Lynn W. "The Electoral Vote Against Monroe in 1820—An American Legend," *Mississippi Valley Historical Review* 42, no. 2 (September 1955).

INDEX

Pages in **boldface** are illustrations.

★ ★ ★ ★ ★ ★ ★ ★ ★ ★ ★ ★ ★ ★ ★ ★ ★

ABOUT THE AUTHORS

Corinne J. Naden is a former U.S. Navy journalist and a children's book editor in New York City. An author of more than eighty-five books for young readers and adults, she lives in Tarrytown, New York.

Rose Blue, a native of Brooklyn, New York, published more than eighty books, fiction and nonfiction, for young readers. Two of them were adapted and aired by NBC television network.